M000076732

The
Language
of
Flowers

The Language of Flowers

Written by
Gail Harvey

~

Designed by
Liz Trovato

Gramercy Books
New York · Avenel

Copyright © 1995 by
Random House Value Publishing, Inc.
All rights reserved

This edition is published by
Gramercy Books,
distributed by
Random House Value Publishing, Inc.
40 Engelhard Avenue
Avenel, New Jersey 07001

New York • Toronto •
London • Sydney • Auckland

Production supervised
by Michael Siebert

Printed and bound
in the United States of America

**Library of Congress
Cataloging-in-Publication Data**
The Language of flowers/
[compiled by] Gail Harvey.
p. cm.
ISBN 0–517–11944–7 : $9.99
1. Flowers–Literary collections.
2. Flowers–Pictorial works.
I. Harvey, Gail, 1942–
PN6071.F5L36 1994
820.8'036–dc20   94–14788
CIP

8 7 6 5 4 3 2 1

Contents

Introduction

It has been said that the language of flowers is as old as the time of Adam and Eve and that the use of floral emblems dates from the first throbbing of love in a human heart. Of all the cultures of which there are reliable records, it is the Greeks who may be considered the earliest florigraphists. They not only had a passionate love of flowers, but they used special blooms for every important occasion, public or private. The minstrel, the poet, the wrestler, and the patriot were all rewarded with appropriate floral wreaths. In Rome, too, a floral crown was considered a fitting guerdon for even the most momentous service. The term "poet laureate" comes from the Roman custom of crowning poets with wreaths of laurel leaves. And it was the Romans who instituted an annual festival in honor of Flora, the goddess of flowers, more than seven hundred years before the birth of Christ.

The language of flowers was well understood and utilized early on in many European countries. In the days when the Catholic faith was preeminent, the significance of flowers was very important. A Catholic was able, for example, to distinguish between fasting and feasting ceremonies by the selection of flowers that adorned the altar. During the Age of Chivalry the knight could manifest his feelings by wearing his lady's colors on his helmet. The lady frequently showed what she felt about his attention by the kind of flowers she wore.

It was Lady Mary Wortley Montagu, wife of the British ambassador to Constantinople, who introduced the Eastern concept of florigraphy to England in 1717. From this an

elaborate language of flowers developed.

The Victorians found the idea of florigraphy irresistible and floral sentiments exactly right for their gentle and unworldly age. No matter how many or how few books a woman might have, she would certainly have the one volume owned by nearly everyone—a floral dictionary containing a list of flowers and the sentiments they expressed.

Florigraphy was considered a science, but one that required little study. According to *Flowers—Their Language and Poetry,* a floral dictionary published in Philadelphia in 1870: "Some flowers almost bear written upon their faces the thoughts of which they are living representatives. That the 'white investments' of the childlike Daisy should, as Shakespeare says, "figure innocence," is self evident; that all nations should select the Rose as an emblem of beauty and love could not be wondered at; whilst the little blue petals of the *Mysotic palustris* require no auger to explain their common name of Forget me not. Who can doubt that the rich perfumes of some plants, or the sparkling lusters of others, must be typical of joy and gladness; or that the melancholy hue and somber looks of others symbolize sadness and despair?"

Although the language of flowers is not difficult to learn, some skill is required to make them into sentences, and much ingenuity may be necessary to explain fully and satisfactorily the sentiments intended to be expressed toward the recipient of the floral message. Victorian couples, who used this fascinating style of correspondence, would frequently agree to use certain secret and original significations known only to themselves, making their charming messages unintelligible to anyone else.

A nineteenth-century writer most eloquently stated: "Flowers have their own language. Theirs is an oratory that speaks in perfumed silence, and there is tenderness, and passion, and even the lightheartedness of mirth, in the variegated beauty of their vocabulary. . . . No spoken word can approach the delicacy of sentiment to be inferred from a flower seasonably offered; the softest expressions may be thus conveyed without offense, and even profound grief alleviated, at a moment when the most tuneful voice would grate harshly on the ear, and when the stricken soul can be soothed only by unbroken silence."

When sending a floral message there are a few basic rules that should be followed, according to the nineteenth-century dictionary. "When a flower is presented in its natural position, the sentiment is to be understood affirmatively; when reversed, negatively. For instance, a rosebud, with its leaves and thorns, indicates fear with hope; but if reversed, it must be construed as saying, "you may neither fear nor hope." Again, divest the same rosebud of its thorns, and it permits the most sanguine hope; deprive it of its petals and retain the thorns, and the worst fears may be entertained. The marigold is emblematic of despair: place it on the head, and it signifies trouble of mind; on the heart, the pangs of love; on the bosom, the despair of weariness and dissatisfaction. The pronoun *I* is expressed by inclining the

symbol to the right, and the pronoun *thou* by inclining it to the left." The position and presentation of flowers is, obviously, crucial. As the Victorians quickly discovered, a mistake could spell the end rather than the beginning of a relationship.

Fruits, vegetables, herbs, spices, and the leaves of trees are also included in the language of flowers. The sentiments expressed by more than one hundred and sixty of these are given in the indices at the end of this book. How thoughtful and imaginative to send a colorful arrangement of fruit that carries a message of congratulations or condolences! A pretty container of nicely arranged herbs and dried spices or a large leaf-lined basket of fresh vegetables might be a charming and useful way to convey feelings of friendship.

This book is a celebration of flowers and the sentiments they express, illustrated with charming Victorian die cuts and lovely paintings by such fine artists as Beatrice Parsons and Edward J. Detmold. Included are tributes to flowers written by some of the world's greatest poets as well as fascinating information about more that fifty popular flowers. You will learn how many of them got their names and what they signify. In addition, you will acquire a new language that can eloquently express your feelings and your changing moods.

GAIL HARVEY

NEW YORK
1995

10

In Eastern lands they talk of flowers,
    And they tell in a garland of their loves and cares;
Each blossom that blooms in their garden bowers
    On its leaves a mystic language bears.

The rose is a sign of joy and love,
    Young blushing love in its earliest dawn;
And the mildness that suits the gentle dove,
    From the myrtle's snowy flower is drawn.

Innocence shines in the lily's bell,
    Pure as the heart in its native heaven;
Fame's bright star and glory's swell,
    By the glossy leaf of the bay are given.

The silent soft and humble heart,
    In the violet's hidden sweetness breathes;
And the tender soul that cannot part,
    A twine of evergreen fondly wreathes.

The cypress that daily shades the grave,
    In sorrow that mourns her bitter lot;
And faith, that a thousand ills can brave,
    And speaks in thy blue leaves—forget-me-not.

Then, gather a wreath from the garden bowers,
And tell the wish of thy heart in flowers.

                                        JAMES GATES PERCIVAL

The Language of Flowers

Almond Blossom

~

INDISCRETION

THOUGHTLESSNESS

The almond tree flowers so early that its beautiful pink or white blossoms are often injured by frost and it bears no fruit that year. This explains why, in the language of flowers, the almond blossom signifies "indiscretion" or "thoughtlessness."

Greek mythologists ascribe the origin of the almond tree to Phyllis, a beautiful young Thracian queen who married Demophoon, with whom she was passionately in love. The son of Theseus and Phaedra, he had been cast by a storm upon the shores of Thrace when he was returning from the siege of Troy. Recalled to Athens when his father died, Demophoon promised to return in a month. One month passed and then another and Phyllis gradually lost all hope of seeing him again. Finally, she died of grief and the gods transformed her body into an almond tree. When Demophoon returned after an absence of three months, he was overcome with sorrow when he learned that his beloved wife was dead. As he wept near the almond tree it put forth flowers as if to prove that she loved him, even after death.

According to Greek mythology, Anemone was a nymph beloved by Zephyr, the god of the west wind. Flora, the goddess of flowers, was jealous of Anemone's beauty and transformed her into a flower, which always blooms at the return of spring. Zephyr abandoned this unfortunate beauty to the rude caresses of Boreas, the god of the north wind, who, unable to gain her love, shakes her until her blossoms are half open, then the lovely colors of her petals begin to fade.

Anemone

~

FORSAKEN

Thy subtle charm is strangely given,
My fancy will not let thee be,
Then poise not thus 'twixt earth and heaven,
O white anemone!

ELAINE GOODALE

Apple Blossom

~

PREFERENCE

The apple blossoms' shower of pearl,
Though blent with rosier hue,
As beautiful as a woman's blush,
As evanescent, too.

L. E. LANDON

What if you have seen it before,
ten thousand times over? An
apple tree in full blossom is like
a message, sent fresh from heaven
to earth, of purity and beauty!

HENRY WARD BEECHER

There is, perhaps, nothing more enchanting than the apple tree in early spring when it is clad in its beautiful blooms. The apple blossom signifies "preference" because it may be preferred to the rose since the lovely flower holds the promise of the delicious fruit to come. The Romans valued the apple tree for its ornamental effect. They considered, justifiably, that the earliness and beauty of the tree's blossoms, as well as the brilliant hues of its fruit, made it a splendid addition to their magnificent gardens.

The aster, which is also called starwort, derives its name from the Greek word *aster*, meaning star. It is said to symbolize "afterthought" because it begins to bloom in late summer and early autumn after other flowers have faded.

The aster was brought to Europe from China, in 1730, by a French missionary. As a result of careful cultivation, today there are many varieties of this showy, remarkably vivid flower, thus explaining why it also signifies "love of variety."

Aster

~

AFTERTHOUGHT
LOVE OF VARIETY

The autumn wood the aster knows,
The empty nest, the wind that grieves,
The sunlight breaking thro' the shade,
The squirrel chattering overhead,
The timid rabbits lighter tread
Among the rustling leaves.

DORA READ GOODALE

Calla
~
MAGNIFICENT BEAUTY

The calla is a member of the lily family. A native of Ethiopia it is much admired for its lovely snow-white calyx, broad green leaves, and pleasant perfume. A flower of magnificent beauty, the calla is often included in a bride's bouquet.

The camellia, also known as the rose of Japan, is one of the loveliest flowers ever introduced into North America. In the language of flowers it signifies "supreme loveliness" as well as "You rule my heart." The camellia was first introduced into Europe in 1639 by a Jesuit monk, Joseph Kamel, from whom it derives its name. Unfortunately, despite its supreme loveliness, this flower has no fragrance.

Camellia

~

SUPREME LOVELINESS

Candytuft

~

INDIFFERENCE

This is a pretty garden flower which bears clusters of small white, pink, or purple blossoms. The first specimens of this plant, a member of the mustard family, were brought from Candia, in Greece, thus explaining its English name. It has a long blooming season and is quite impervious to inclement weather, which is, undoubtedly, why it symbolizes "indifference."

Canterbury Bell

~

CONSTANCY

GRATITUDE

A member of the *Campanula*, or bell, family, the canterbury bell was so named because it grew in such profusion in the English city of Canterbury. Some florigraphists claim that this flower signifies "constancy," others say that it is the emblem of "gratitude." The deep purple bells are generally very large, but there is a variety that has blue, purple, or white bells that are smaller. It is easy to imagine these tiny trembling bells ringing merrily for the benefit of such elves as lurk "under the blossom that hangs on the bough."

The significance of the carnation changes according to its color. While the striped carnation is the emblem of "refusal," the red carnation signifies "Alas for my poor heart," and the yellow carnation is the symbol of "disdain."

There are many myths about the carnation's origin. According to one story, the carnation grew in Paradise. Another suggests that it sprang from the graves of young lovers. The carnation is among the oldest flowers to be cultivated. It was known in Britain in the fourteenth century and was mentioned by Chaucer. It is believed that its name derives from Incarnacyon. The carnation has a strong religious association as is obvious from many of the names by which it has been known—the Passion, drops of Christ's blood, and divine flower.

The story is told that Marie Antoinette, imprisoned in Paris in 1793, wrote an escape plan on a tiny piece of paper which she hid in the calyx of a striped carnation and sent to friends. The note was intercepted and she went to the guillotine two months later.

Carnation

~

REFUSAL

Chrysanthemum

CHEERFULNESS
IN ADVERSITY

*In the second month the peach
tree blooms, but not until the ninth
the chrysanthemums: so each must
wait until his own time comes.*

AN OLD CHINESE PROVERB

The chrysanthemum has been bred for centuries by gardeners in China and Japan, where the plant originated. Although this flower was cultivated by the Chinese as early as 500 B.C., they were not successfully introduced to Europe until the end of the eighteenth century. When almost all other flowers have stopped blooming and the wind and rain of autumn have begun, the chrysanthemum blooms. In October and the dismal month of November some varieties are at the peak of their perfection. The chrysanthemum quite appropriately signifies "cheerfulness in adversity."

Columbine
~
FOLLY

A native of North America, the columbine is a graceful and pretty flower that grows in open places in the forest and on rocky hillsides. The blooms may be scarlet, pink, purple, or white and make a handsome addition to the garden. It is difficult to say why the columbine has come to signify "folly." Some claim it is because the shape of its nectary is similar to that of a jester's cap.

Cornflower
~
DELICACY

From earliest times, artists have pounded the deep blue petals of the cornflower to make a delicate blue paint. The classic name of this blossom is *Cyanus.* It was so named after a fair young devotee of Flora, the goddess of flowers. For public festivals, Cyanus made garlands from a variety of wildflowers and spent many happy hours in the cornfields, singing softly as she wove the blossoms she had collected into delicate crowns and decorations. One day, Flora found Cyanus lying dead in the cornfield and transformed her into the cornflower as a tribute to her devoted love.

Crocus

~

CHEERFULNESS

Welcome, wild harbinger of spring!
    To this small nook of earth;
Feeling and fancy fondly cling
    Round thoughts which owe their birth
To thee, and to the humble spot
Where chance has fixed thy lowly lot.

BERNARD BARTON

Some authorities say that this charming little flower, which heralds the spring, derives its name from a Greek word which means "thread" because saffron is derived from its stamen, or thread. Greek legend has it that the gods took pity on an unhappy lover named Crocus and transformed him into the bright and cheerful flower that bears his name.

Cyclamen

~

DIFFIDENCE

The Romans called the cyclamen *tuber terrae* because of its turnip-like root. In the seventeenth century the fresh tubers were made into an ointment and applied to the skin to prevent disfiguring pitting after smallpox. In addition to being fed to pigs, the tubers were ground and made into cakes which were eaten for their supposed healthful and aphrodisiac properties. The cyclamen signifies "diffidence" because it never raises its head to the sun.

Thou Cyclamen of crumpled horn
  Toss not thy head aside;
Repose it where the Loves were born
  In that warm dell abide.
Whatever flowers, on mountain, field,
  Or garden, may arise,
Thine only that pure odor yield
  Which never can suffice.
Emblem of her I've loved so long,
  Go, carry her this little song.
                    WALTER SAVAGE LANDOR

Daffodil

UNREQUITED LOVE

The daffodil, the yellow-colored species of the narcissus, is much loved by writers and poets. It is said to be the flower that Proserpine was gathering when Pluto, the Greek god of the underworld, seized her and carried her off to the dark infernal regions. Dis was Pluto's counterpart in Roman mythology and, since early writers regarded this flower as a member of the lily family, it is quite possible that its name is simply a corruption of Dis's lily. It has also been known as daffidowndilly, dafflily, and chalice flower.

She stepped upon Sicilian grass,
*   Demeter's daughter fresh and fair,*
A child of light, a radiant lass,
*   And gamesome as the morning air.*
The daffodils were fair to see,
*   They nodded lightly o'er the lea.*

JEAN INGELOW

I wandered, lonely as a cloud
That floats on high o'er vales and hills,
When all at once I saw a crowd—
A host of golden daffodils
Beside the lake, beneath the trees,
Flutt'ring and dancing in the breeze.

Continuous as the stars that shine
And twinkle on the milky way,
They stretched in never-ending line
Along the margin of a bay:
Ten thousand saw I, at a glance,
Tossing their heads in sprightly dance.

The waves beside them danced, but they
Outdid the sparkling waves in glee:
A poet could not but be gay,
In such a jocund company;
I gazed—and gazed—but little thought
What wealth the show to me had brought:

For oft, when on my couch I lie,
In vacant or in pensive mood,
They flash upon that inward eye
Which is the bliss of solitude,
And then my heart with pleasure fills,
And dances with the daffodils.

WILLIAM WORDSWORTH

Dahlia
~
DIGNITY

ELEGANCE

*The dahlias will blossom by the last of
June, unfolding their large rich stars in
great abundance till frost. They blossom
in every variety of color except blue;
all shades of red from faint rose to
black-maroon, and all are gold-centered.
They are every shade of yellow from
sulphur to flame—king's flowers,
I call them, stately and splendid.*

CELIA THAXTER

The dahlia is a native of Mexico. It was brought
to Spain in 1789 and adorned the royal garden
for nine years before the Spanish would permit
it to be introduced into the other countries of
Europe where it astonished English travelers
with its profusion and delighted them with its
brilliance. The dahlia was named after Andrew
Dahl, a Swedish botanist. He presented it in
1804 to Lady Holland, the first person to successfully cultivate the flower in England.

Perhaps because the dahlia has no scent,
and some feel that its foliage is coarse and its
flowers gaudy, it has attracted no poetic tributes.

The daisy is the flower which, next to the rose, seems to have received the most attention from the poets. According to legend, this little flower owes its origin to Belides, one of the nymphs who presided over woodlands. It is said that one day when Belides was dancing with Ephigeus, her favored suitor, she attracted the attention of Vertumnus, the god of orchards. To protect her from his pursuit, Flora, the goddess of flowers, transformed her into Bellis, the daisy. One of the great Gaelic poets claimed a more celestial origin for this pretty flower. He wrote that the daisy was first sown above a baby's grave by the dimpled hands of infant angels.

The English name of daisy is derived from a Saxon word meaning day's eye, probably because the blossom opens at daybreak and closes at sunset.

The following poem was written by an unknown author:

> I'd choose to be a daisy,
>   If I might be a flower,
> Closing my petals softly
>   At twilight's quiet hour;
> And waking in the morning,
>   When falls the early dew,
> To welcome Heaven's bright sunshine,
>   And Heaven's bright teardrops, too.

Daisy
~
INNOCENCE

> With little here to do or see
> Of things that in the great world be,
> Daisy! again I talk to thee,
>   For thou art worthy;
> Thou unassuming commonplace
> Of Nature, with that homely face,
> And yet with something of a grace,
>   Which love makes for thee!
>
> WILLIAM WORDSWORTH

Dandelion

You cannot forget if you would those golden kisses all over the cheeks of the meadow, queerly called dandelions.

HENRY WARD BEECHER

This common little wild flower is not only extremely useful for many culinary and medicinal purposes. Because of its presumed oracular powers many a bright young eye has been made to gleam brighter or to dim with tears of foreboding; for it is this golden-petaled blossom that is often selected to decide whether "he loves me" or "he loves me not." The dandelion is not, however, considered an oracle only on matters of the heart. In addition, because the blossom opens and closes at regular hours, it has long served the solitary shepherd as a clock.

The English name of this flower seems to have derived from the name it was given in French. Because of the deeply notched edges of the dandelion's leaves, which were thought to resemble the teeth of a lion, the flower was called *dent de lion,* or lion-toothed.

Dear common flower, that grow'st beside the way
Fringing the dusty road with harmless gold,
First pledge of blithesome May,
Which children pluck, and full of pride uphold,
High-hearted buccaneers, o'erjoyed that they
An Eldorado in the grass have found,
Which not the rich earth's ample round
May match in wealth, thou art more dear to me
Than all the prouder summer blooms may be.

JAMES RUSSELL LOWELL

Delphinium

LIGHTNESS

The lovely delphinium signifies "lightness" because of the graceful airiness of the flowers. According to legend, this flower arose from the blood of Ajax, the Trojan warrior. Disappointed in a division of the spoils after one of his battles, the hot-tempered Ajax rushed into the open and wreaked his anger on a flock of sheep, stabbing several with his sword before he recovered from his madness. Ashamed of the spectacle he had made of himself, he turned his sword on himself and perished. His blood poured into the earth, then flowered into the air again as the *delphinium Ajacis.*

Some people claim that the flower got its name from its supposed resemblance to the spur on a dolphin's head. But the shape of the flower has suggested many things to many eyes, for it is also known as larkspur because of its likeness to the spur on a lark's claw.

Delphinium have been cultivated since the time of the Pharaohs, when they were considered important plants because it was believed that the seeds had the ability to destroy vermin.

Evening Primrose

~

INCONSTANCY
SILENT LOVE

When the sun sinks in the west,
And dew-drops pearl the evening's
breast;
Almost as pale as moonbeams are,
Or its companionable star,
The Evening Primrose opes anew
The delicate blossoms to the dew;
And hermit-like, shunning the light,
Wastes its fair bloom upon the night;
Who, blindfold to its fond caresses,
Knows not the beauty he possesses.
Thus it blooms on while night is by;
When day looks out with open eye,
'Bashed at the gaze it cannot shun,
It faints, and withers, and is gone.

JOHN CLARE

The evening primrose does not open her cup of pale gold until the moon has risen. This flower looks up at the silvery moon and often by midnight is surrounded by many of the insects who avoid daylight and resort to her for their nightly banquet. When the nights are dark, and not the slightest breath of air is stirring, the petals emit a mild phosphoric light and look almost as if they have been lit for a holiday.

Forget Me Not

~

TRUE LOVE

There is a German legend that accounts for the name of this beautiful little blue flower, as well as for its significance in the language of flowers. One day a young knight and his sweetheart were walking on the banks of the Danube. The young lady saw a bunch of blue flowers floating down the river. "I must have that pretty bouquet," she cried. Her chivalrous suitor immediately plunged into the river and caught the flowers. But, alas, encumbered by the weight of his armor he was unable to climb the river's slippery bank. Despite all his efforts he found himself sinking quickly. He flung the bouquet ashore to his sweetheart and, with his last breath, as he sank forever, he called to her, "Forget me not!"

With such a romantic tragedy attached to it, it is not surprising that so many poetic tributes have been paid to this small heavenly blue flower.

The sweet forget-me-nots,
That grow for happy lovers.
ALFRED, LORD TENNYSON

Dear girl, I send this spray of flowers—
All withered now, once brightest blue—
To call to mind those happy hours,
Those happy hours I passed with you.
Forget me not! that might have been
The answer to my fervid prayers.
JOHN INGRAM

The blue and bright-eyed floweret
of the brook,
Hope's gentle gem, the sweet
forget-me-not.
SAMUEL COLERIDGE

Foxglove
∽
INSINCERITY

This beautiful flower is emblematic of "insincerity" because at the time that the language of flowers was conceived it was said that an invidious poison lurked within its bright blossoms. Today that poison, digitalis, is extracted from the plant and used as a cardiac stimulant and a diuretic.

The foxglove varies in color from a deep purple to a violet hue as well as a tawny orange, blush pink, white, and cream. The inside of the inversely conical bells are speckled, which adds to their richness. Alfred, Lord Tennyson described quite accurately "the foxglove's dappled bells."

Fuchsia
∽
TASTE

The fuchsia, a native of Chile, was named in honor of Leonard Fuchs, the noted sixteenth-century German botanist. This hardy plant blooms from July until frost. The flowers are stunning. Some varieties are pink and white, others are scarlet and violet, and, perhaps the most spectacular, bright crimson and purple. The fuchsia has many popular names including rose of Castile, sophisticated lady, and party gown, which might explain why it signifies "taste."

This lovely autumn wildflower is a glorious deep blue and has delicately fringed petals. It bears the name of Geneus, the king of Illyria, who discovered that the plant was useful in treating various ills. Physicians of old did use the plant to treat ailments as diverse as dog bites, stubborn livers, weariness, lameness, and pestilences. In Hungary the plant was known as *Sanctus Ladislas Regis Herba,* in honor of Ladislas, the king, whose reign was greatly troubled by a plague. In despair, Ladislas went into the fields carrying his bow and arrow. He prayed that when he shot at random the Lord would direct the arrow to a plant that might be of use in checking the ravages of the terrible disease. He shot the arrow and it was found sticking into a root of gentian, which he immediately picked, and with which wondrous cures were wrought. None of this would seem to explain, however, why this unusual blue flower came to signify "virgin pride."

Gentian
~
VIRGIN PRIDE

Thou blossom, bright with autumn dew,
And colored with the heaven's own blue,
That openest when the quiet light
Succeeds the keen and frosty night;

Thou comest not when violets lean
O'er wandering brooks and springs unseen,
Or columbines, in purple dressed,
Nod o'er the ground-bird's hidden nest.

Thou waitest late, and com'st alone,
When woods are bare and birds are flown,
And frosts and shortening days portend
The aged Year is near his end.

Then doth thy sweet and quiet eye
Look through thy fringes to the sky,
Blue-blue-as if that sky let fall
A flower from its cerulean wall.

I would that thus, when I shall see
The hour of death draw near to me,
Hope, blossoming within my heart,
May look to heaven as I depart.

WILLIAM CULLEN BRYANT

Geranium

~

PREFERENCE

There are as many florigraphic meanings to the geranium as there are varieties. The popular rose- or pink-scented variety is symbolic of "preference." Many species of geranium or, more properly, of pelargonium, were introduced to England from South Africa in the eighteenth and nineteenth centuries. The name geranium is derived from the Greek and means crane, since the flower's carpel, or fruit, has a long and noticeable beak.

The scented geranium signifies preference because of the softness of its leaves, the beauty of the bloom, and its fragrant perfume. The leaf emits a delightful scent when it is lightly rubbed with a finger.

The scarlet geranium, which is not only the most common, but also the most popular geranium, is, strangely, recorded in the language of flowers as the emblem of "stupidity."

If the rose is the favorite flower of the world's poets, the richly scented snowy blossoms of the hawthorn have been the great love of British bards. Symbolizing "hope," the hawthorn has been lauded by poets, beginning with Chaucer, and beloved by the people. In olden days the tree was known by the name May, because that was the month when it burst into bloom. Houses and churches were decorated on May Day with the scented blossoms. In the country it was the custom for young men and women to get up soon after midnight on the first of May and, accompanied by musicians, to walk to a wood where they gathered as many branches and bouquets of hawthorn as they could carry. They returned home at sunrise in a joyous procession, garlanded with flowers and laden with blossomy boughs with which to decorate the village.

   The common color of these delicate blossoms is white, frequently blushed with pink, but there is a garden variety with double flowers of deep red.

Gives not the hawthorn bush a sweeter shade
To shepherds, looking on their silly sheep,
Than doth a rich embroidered canopy
To kings that fear their subjects treachery?
                                    WILLIAM SHAKESPEARE

Hawthorn
~
HOPE

And every shepherd tells his tale
Under the hawthorn in the dale.
                        JOHN MILTON

Holly

FORESIGHT

With its shining green foliage and brilliant red berries, holly always brightens the dull winter landscape. In frost, in snow, in sun, or rain, holly's glossy leaves are always shining brightly, bringing renewed hope to all who see them. It was once believed that a holly hedge around a house was protection against poison, the evil eye, storms, and fire. The custom of using holly to decorate at Christmas comes from the Roman festival of Saturn, which was celebrated in December. According to legend, the first holly sprang up under the footsteps of Christ. Medieval monks called holly the Holy Tree. They said that the sharp spines on the leaves represented the Crown of Thorns, the white flowers were emblematic of purity and the birth of Christ, the red berries represented drops of His blood, and the bitter bark was symbolic of the Passion.

All green was vanished save of pine and yew,
That still displayed their melancholy hue;
Save the green holly with its berries red,
And the green moss that o'er the gravel spread.

GEORGE CRABBE

Hollyhock

FRUITFULNESS

It is said that this superb and hardy plant was brought to Europe from Syria at the time of the Crusades. Because the hollyhock produces so many luscious flowers on each stalk it is appropriate that it should symbolize "fruitfulness." Celia Thaxter, who was particularly fond of hollyhocks, wrote in her book *An Island Garden:* "One enormous red hollyhock grew thirteen feet high last year. Oh, but he was superb! At night the lights from one window. . . illumined him as he swayed to and fro in the wind, a stately column of beauty and grace. A black-red comrade leaned against him and mingled its rich blossoms with his brighter color, and near him were rose, pink, and cherry, and white spikes of bloom, lovely to behold."

Honeysuckle

BONDS OF LOVE

The honeysuckle often amorously attaches its pliant branches to the trunk of a tree, adorning its friendly supporter with elegant festoons and perfumed garlands. It is, therefore, quite appropriate that honeysuckle has come to signify "bonds of love."

Fair flower, that does so comely grow,
  Hid in this silent, dull retreat,
Untouched thy honeyed blossoms blow,
  Unseen thy little branches greet:
    No roving foot shall crush thee here,
    No busy hand provoke a tear.

By Nature's self in white arrayed,
  She bade thee shun the vulgar eye,
And planted here the guardian shade,
  And sent soft waters murmuring by
    Thus quietly thy summer goes—
    Thy days declining to repose.

From morning suns and evening dews
  At first thy little being came:
If nothing once, you nothing lose,
  For when you die you are the same;
    The space between is but an hour,
    The frail duration of a flower.

PHILIP FRENEAU

The hyacinth, which comes from the Mediterranean, has elegantly shaped bell blossoms which tower one above the other upon graceful stems. A group of these lovely flowers, in nearly every color of the rainbow, is a glorious spectacle.

According to mythologists, this highly scented, fragile flower had its origin in the death of Hyacinthus, a handsome prince who was greatly favored by Apollo, the god of sunlight, and fell victim to the jealous rage of Zephyr, the god of the west wind, who was determined to destroy him. One day when Hyacinthus and Apollo were playing quoits, Zephyr blew so powerfully upon the ring of iron flung by Apollo that it struck the young man on the temple and killed him. Apollo, the innocent slayer, was overcome with grief. Unable to restore the prince to life, he caused the flower, which now bears his name, to spring from his blood. This is the reason that the hyacinth, so celebrated in the songs of the poets, beginning with Homer, came to signify "play." It would certainly be thought, however, that a more sober meaning should have been attributed to a flower which was said to have had such a sad origin.

The hyacinth purple, and white, and blue,
Which flung from its bells a sweet peal anew.
Of music, so delicate, soft, and intense,
It was felt like an odor within the sense.

PERCY BYSSHE SHELLEY

Hyacinth
~
PLAY

39

Iris

~

I Have a Message
for Thee

Every varying hue
Of every beautiful thing on earth—the tints
Of heaven's own Iris—all are in the west
On this delicious eve.

John Carrington

There are more than two hundred species of the beautiful iris. Their colors include pale sky-blue, many hues of purple, as well as yellow and white. It is because of these brilliant and varied colors, resembling those of the rainbow, that this sweet flower has been named after Iris, the Greek goddess and a messenger of the gods. It is well known that the lovely Iris was the bearer of only good news.

Also known as flower-de-luce, or flower of light, the three petals of the iris are said to represent faith, wisdom, and valor. The yellow iris symbolizes "flame" and "passion of love."

Thou art the Iris, fair among the fairest,
Who, armed with golden rod
And winged with the celestial azure,
Bearest the message of some God.

Thou art the Muse, who far from crowded cities
Hauntest the sylvan streams,
Playing on pipes of reed the artless ditties
That come to us as dreams.

O flower-de-luce, bloom on, and let the river
Linger to kiss thy feet!
O flower of song, bloom on, and make forever
The world more frail and sweet.

Henry Wadsworth Longfellow

40

The ivy shuns the city wall,
Where busy, clamorous crowds intrude,
And climbs the desolated hall
In silent solitude;
The time-worn arch, the fallen dome,
Are roots for its eternal home.

JOHN CLARE

From behind the roof
Rose the slim ash and mossy sycamore,
Blending their diverse foliage with the green
Of ivy, flourishing and thick, that clasped
The huge round chimneys, harbor of delight
For wren and redbreast, where they sit and sing
Their slender ditties when the trees are bare.

WILLIAM WORDSWORTH

Ivy

FRIENDSHIP
WEDDED LOVE
MARRIAGE

In ancient Greece, the altar of Hymen was surrounded with ivy, a sprig of which the priest presented to each newly married spouse as a symbol of an indissoluble knot. In addition to ivy's significance as "marriage," it is also appropriately the emblem of "friendship" and of "wedded love" since nothing is able to separate the ivy from the tree around which it has entwined itself. It clothes the tree with its own foliage, within which it often shelters small birds. The ivy, which has rather insignificant green flowers and black berries, is by no means a parasitical plant since its roots are firmly fixed in the earth.

Jasmine

~

AMIABILITY

The significance of jasmine depends on its color. The fragrant white jasmine is emblematic of "amiability," the yellow signifies "grace and elegance." The pinkish red jasmine is a token of "separation." Indian jasmine, the blossoms of which are bright yellow, large, and heavily scented, is called champaca and represents "the sweetness of friendship."

The favorite is Spanish jasmine, so called because it is believed to have been introduced to Europe in 1560 by Spaniards who brought it from the East Indies. The petals of the flower are a blush-red outside and pale blush pink within. It symbolizes "sensuality." The common white jasmine is, however, an exceedingly elegant plant and is not surpassed in fragrance or beauty by any other species.

Lavender

~

MISTRUST

Since ancient times lavender has been valued for its refreshing fragrance. The Romans, who believed it relieved fatigue and the soreness of muscles, used lavender flowers to perfume their baths. (Its name comes from the French word *lavare,* which means "to wash.") But the lavender plant was always approached with some trepidation because it was believed to be a favorite hiding place of the deadly asp. Consequently, it was never used in wreaths and garlands and came to signify "mistrust." Herbalists, however, recommended lavender to relieve aches and pains. And for centuries dried lavender has been used to ward off moths and to perfume linens.

Lilac

~

FIRST EMOTION
OF LOVE
YOUTHFUL INNOCENCE

The lilac, various in array, now white,
Now sanguine, and her beauteous head
*   now set*
With purple spikes pyramidal, as if
Studious of ornament, yet unresolved
Which hue she most approved, she chose
*   them all.*

WILLIAM COWPER

The lilac comes from Persia where it was called *lilag,* or flower. It was taken to Europe early in the sixteenth century and brought to North America by the pilgrims. To many people the lilac was a flower of ill luck—a result of the association of its purple color with the hues of mourning. According to an old proverb "She who wears lilacs will never wear a wedding ring." It was once a custom to send a spray of lilac to a lover as a sensitive way of saying the relationship was over. This may have been inspired by the story of an English nobleman who seduced an innocent young woman and then abandoned her. She died of a broken heart. Her friends put a wreath of purple lilac on her grave that, overnight, turned white and soon grew into a large shrub. This, the first white lilac, is still pointed out in the church-yard of a hamlet on the Wye, in Hartfordshire.

Today, however, the purple lilac signifies the "first emotions of love" because nothing is more delightful than the sensations it produces when spring returns and the lilac first appears. Bursting into a profusion of fragrant bouquet-shaped blossoms, the purple lilac could scarcely escape being chosen by the observant poet and lover as a symbol of those feelings of joy which bloom when first love shyly manifests itself.

Because of the purity and short duration of the delicate flowers of the sweetly scented white lilac, it has become the symbol of youth; of that fleet and enchanting time which money cannot buy, nor power retain or restore.

I am thinking of the lilac trees,
　　That shook their purple plumes,
And when the sash was open,
　　Shed fragrance through the room.

ANNA S. STEPHENS

O were my Love you lilac fair,
　　Wi' purple blossoms to the spring,
And I a bird to shelter there,
　　When wearied on my little wing;
How I wad mourn when it was torn
　　By autumn wild and winter rude!
But I wad sing on wanton wing
　　When youthfu' May its bloom renew'd.

ROBERT BURNS

Lily

PURITY

I like not lady slippers,
Nor yet the sweet-pea blossoms,
Nor yet the flaky roses,
  Red or white or snow;
I like the chaliced lilies,
The heavy Eastern lilies,
The gorgeous tiger lilies,
  That in our garden grow.
T. B. ALDRICH

Throughout history the magnificent white lily has been regarded as the symbol of purity. According to one legend, the first lily sprang from the tears of Eve as she went from the Garden of Eden. Long before Christianity, however, the Romans and Greeks held the white lily in high regard. This lovely flower is dedicated to the Virgin Mary. When doubting Thomas insisted that her tomb be opened to see if she had really been resurrected, he found it filled with roses and beautiful white lilies. Since the lily comes into bloom about the time of the Annunciation it is always used to decorate the altar of the Virgin.

In the language of flowers other lilies have different meanings. The Arum lily, for example, signifies "ardor." The tiger lily sends the message, "For once may pride befriend me," and the yellow day lily is the emblem of "coquetry."

And the stately lilies stand
Fair in the silvery light,
Like saintly vestals, pale in prayer;
Their pure breath sanctifies the air,
As its fragrance fills the night.

JULIA C. R. DORE

We are Lilies fair,
The flower of virgin light;
Nature held us forth, and said,
"Lo! my thoughts of white."

LEIGH HUNT

And the wandlike lily which lifted up,
As a Maenad, its moonlight-colored cup,
Till the fiery star, which is its eye,
Gazed through clear dew on the tender sky.

PERCY BYSSHE SHELLEY

Lily of the Valley
~
RETURN OF HAPPINESS

The lily of the valley signifies the "return of happiness" because in May, soon after spring has returned, it puts forth its perfumed blossoms. This sweet plant, which loves the shelter of a hollow valley, the shade of an oak, or the cool bank of a stream, has had many poetic tributes.

No flower amid the garden fairer grows
Than the sweet lily of the lowly vale,
The queen of flowers.
JOHN KEATS

That shy plant—the lily of the vale,
That loves the ground, and from the sun withholds
Her pensive beauty, from the breeze her sweets.
WILLIAM WORDSWORTH

The lily of the vale, of flowers the queen,
Puts on the robe she neither sewed nor spun.
MICHAEL BRUCE

This superb emblem of "magnificence" was named in honor of Pierre Magnol, a well-known writer on botanical subjects. A native of the southern United States, the magnolia tree begins to blossom in May and continues to flower, perfuming the air for many months.

Magnolia

MAGNIFICENCE

Majestic flower! How purely beautiful
Thou art, as rising from the bower
of green,
Those dark and glossy leaves so thick
and full,
Thou standest like a high-born
forest queen
Among thy maidens clustering round
so fair,
I love to watch thy sculptured form
unfolding,
And look into thy depths, to image there
A fairy cavern, and while thus
beholding,
And while thy breeze floats o'er thee,
matchless flower,
I breathe the perfume, delicate and
strong,
That comes like incense from thy
petal-bower;
My fancy roams those southern
woods along,
Beneath that glorious tree, where
deep among
The unsunned leaves thy large white
flower-cups hung!

C. P. CRANCH

Marigold
~
GRIEF
DESPAIR

The marigold, whose courtier's face
Echoes the sun, and doth unlace
Her at his rise, at his full stop
Packs and shuts up her gaudy shop.

JOHN CLEVELAND

When with a serious musing I behold
The graceful and obsequious marigold,
How duly every morning she displays
Her open breast, when Titan spreads
his rays.

GEORGE WITHER

The classic name for this flower is *Calendula*, which some writers translate into the "flower of all the months" because it is in bloom for so many months of the year. Old English poets called the flower "gold." Since, in the Middle Ages, the name of the Virgin Mary was a frequent addition to the name of anything useful or beautiful, this flower became know as the "marygold."

It is difficult to understand why so dazzling a flower should have come to signify "grief" and "despair," but in many countries it is so regarded. When Charles I, for example, was held prisoner in Carisbrooke Castle he wrote:

The marigold observes the sun
More than my subjects me have done.

The marigold's sorrowful sentiments can, however, be tempered by using it with other flowers. Combined with roses, it is symbolic of "the bitter sweets and pleasant pains of love." And in the Far East a bouquet of marigolds and poppies signifies "I will allay your pain."

Myrtle
~
LOVE

The myrtle, like the rose, is symbolic of "love." The Romans consecrated it to Venus, the goddess of love and beauty, around whose temples they planted myrtle groves. According to mythologists, when Venus sprang from the foam of the sea the houris crowned her with a wreath of myrtle. Once, when she was surprised by a group of satyrs as she emerged from her bath, she found shelter behind the thick foliage of the myrtle.

Not only was this plant surrounded with the sanctity of love, but its beauty and fragrance made it a favorite of many ancient peoples. In the Old Testament myrtle is a symbol of peace. The Arabs say that when Adam was expelled from Paradise he brought the myrtle into the world with him. And Athenian magistrates wore chaplets of myrtle as symbols of their authority.

The blossoms of the myrtle are particularly beautiful, but even when the shrub is flowerless the deep lustrous green of its foliage is much admired.

See, rooted in the earth,
her kindly bed,
The unendangered myrtle,
decked with flowers,
Before the threshold stands
to welcome us!
WILLIAM WORDSWORTH

Goddess, I do love a girl,
Ruby-lipped and toothed with pearl.
If so be I may but prove
Lucky in this maid I love,
I will promise there shall be
Myrtles offered up to thee.
ROBERT HERRICK

Narcissus

SELF-LOVE
EGOTISM

The white narcissus is aptly considered the florigraphic sign of "self-
love," or "egotism," since according to
mythology it owes its origin to a
handsome young man named
Narcissus. It had been foretold that
he would live happily until he beheld
his own face. One warm day
Narcissus had been out hunting and
was very thirsty. He stopped at a
stream to get some water. In so doing
he saw the reflection of his handsome face and immediately fell in
love with his own image. The nymph
Echo, in retribution for his rejection
of her, persuaded the gods to change
him into the flower that now bears
his name.

The narcissus, often called the
poetic narcissus, has quite flat snow-
white petals, with a yellow cup in the
center, fringed on the border with a
brilliant crimson circlet. It has a
sweet scent and flowers in May. The
central cup is said to contain the tears
of the ill-fated Narcissus.

The brightly colored flower of the nasturtium, as well as the leaves, are shaped like helmets and shields, which, perhaps, explains why it signifies "patriotism." The nasturtium is a North American plant and for centuries its flowers and leaves, which have a peppery taste, were used as salad ingredients as, indeed, they often are today.

Nasturtium
~
Patriotism

Pansy

~

REMEMBRANCE

YOU OCCUPY
MY THOUGHTS

The pansy's name comes from the French *pensée,* which means "thought" or "heart's ease," thus its significance of "remembrance" and "you occupy my thoughts." The pansy has lovely diversifications and contrasts of color and its petals have a glossy velvet sheen. "There are pansies: that's for thoughts," wrote William Shakespeare and described the pansy as originally milk-white, until it was struck by an arrow that Cupid had aimed at Diana, so that now it is "purple with love's wounds."

I send thee pansies while the year is young,
  Yellow as sunshine, purple as the night;
Flowers of remembrance, ever fondly sung
  By all the chiefest of the Sons of Light;
And if in recollection lives regret
  For wasted days and dreams that were not true,
I tell thee that the "pansy freak'd with jet"
  Is still the heart's ease that the poets knew
Take all the sweetness of a gift unsought,
And for the pansies send me back a thought.

SARAH DOWDNEY

The beauteous pansies rise
  In purple, gold, and blue,
With tints of rainbow hue
  Mocking the sunset skies.

THOMAS J. OUSELEY

Heart's ease! one could look for half a day
Upon this flower, and shape in fancy out
Full twenty different tales of love and sorrow,
That gave this gentle name.

MARY HOWITT

Peony

SHAME

The peony, among the earliest known medicinal plants, was named after Paeon, the legendary physician to the gods of ancient Greece. It was once believed that the peony, in addition to having marvelous curative properties, had the power to repel evil spirits and storms and could bestow long life. It is difficult to understand why these magnificent perennials, which have large pink, deep red, or white flowers, should signify "shame." Perhaps it is because it was believed that wearing a necklace of peony seeds would counter such "shameful" diseases as leprosy, epilepsy, lunacy, and chronic nightmares.

The delicate blue of the periwinkle harmonizes with the shady places where it grows. This small plant attaches itself firmly to the earth, which it adorns. Its pliant branches spread across the ground and are covered with flowers that seem to reflect the color of the sky. In France the periwinkle is considered the emblem of "sincere friendship" and as such it is much used in their language of flowers. To the English this evergreen plant signifies "tender recollections." In Italy the country people make garlands of periwinkles to place upon the biers of their deceased children and for this reason call it the "flower of death." In Germany it is the symbol of "immortality" because the plant's glossy, bright green leaves flourish all through the winter.

Periwinkle

~

TENDER RECOLLECTIONS

SINCERE FRIENDSHIP

Through primrose tufts in that green bower,
The periwinkle trailed its wreaths;
And 'tis my faith that every flower
Enjoys the air it breathes.

WILLIAM WORDSWORTH

Here is the hedge along which the periwinkle breathes and twines so profusely; with its evergreen leaves shining like the myrtle, and its starry blue flowers…when we do meet with it, it is so abundant and so welcome— the very robin-redbreast of flowers, a winter friend.

MARY RUSSELL MITFORD

Poppy

CONSOLATION
OBLIVION

We are slumberous poppies,
Lords of Lethe downs,
Some awake and some asleep,
Sleeping in our crowns.
What perchance our dreams
may know,
Let our serious beauty show.
LEIGH HUNT

According to the language of flowers, the poppy signifies "consolation." This is probably because of the Greek myth which tells us that the poppy was created by Ceres to ameliorate her grief while she searched for her daughter Proserpine. The well-known soporific quality of the poppy is certainly a good reason for it being symbolic of "oblivion," too. Shakespeare and Spenser were among the poets who alluded to the "drowsy poppy" and Leigh Hunt called it the "blissful poppy" because of its soothing and sleep-inducing properties.

I sing the Poppy! The frail snowy week!
The flower of Mercy! that within its heart
Doth keep "a drop serene" for human need,
A drowsy balm for every bitter smart.
For happy hours the Rose will idly blow—
The Poppy hath a charm for pain and woe.
MARY A. BARR

The saffron tufts of the primrose announce the return of spring. The season of cold winds and hoar frost has passed, but the bright warm days of summer have not yet arrived. This flower represents, therefore, the age between childhood and young womanhood and symbolizes "early youth." Its name comes from the Latin *prima rosa,* the first flower of the season.

Until the middle of the seventeenth century the primrose was always a deep yellow. Then gardeners in England began to cultivate the flower in many colors, including deep crimson, lavender, pale yellow, and a vivid scarlet.

Primrose
~
EARLY YOUTH

Primroses, the Spring may love them;
Summer knows but little of them.
WILLIAM WORDSWORTH

Rose

~

LOVE

BEAUTY

Love is like a rose,
The joy of all the earth . . .
CHRISTINA ROSSETTI

What's in a name?
That which we call a rose,
By any other name would
smell as sweet.
WILLIAM SHAKESPEARE

Universally the rose is considered to be the loveliest of all the flowers. There is scarcely a poet of any note in the world of literature who has not paid tribute to this flower. The rose originated in the East, but today it opens its glowing petals to the sun in every quarter of the globe. Its scent is the most exquisite, its colors the most fascinating, and the green of its leaves the most refreshing of all of nature's beauties.

The rose is mentioned by the earliest writers of antiquity. Herodotus, for example, speaks of the double rose. In the Song of Solomon there is a reference to the rose of Sharon, as well as mention of the plantation of roses at Jericho.

The rose has always been associated with love and female beauty. It is said that when Aphrodite, the goddess of love, rose from the sea, the foam which covered her nakedness turned into white rose bushes as it fell to the ground. According to mythologists, Aphrodite also created the red rose. It happened when Adonis, the handsome young man whom she loved, was gored by a wild boar. As she ran to help him she scratched herself on the thorns of a rosebush. It was her blood that turned the white roses to red.

It is the red rose that is the rose of myth and legend. In the Middle Ages, Christians adopted it as the symbol of the blood of martyrs. It is dedicated to the Virgin Mary and the beads of the original rosary, devised by St. Dominic, were made of tightly compressed, fragrant rose petals.

Queen of fragrance, lovely rose,
The beauties of thy leaves disclose!
The winter's past, the tempests fly,
Soft gales breathe gently through the sky;
The lark's sweet warbling on the wing
Salutes the gay return of spring:
The silver dews, the vernal showers,
Call forth a bloomy waste of flowers;
The joyous fields, the shady woods,
Are cloth'd with green, or swell with buds;
Then haste the beauties to disclose,
Queen of fragrance, lovely rose!

WILLIAM BROOME

Go, lovely rose,
Tell her that wastes her time and me,
    That now she knows,
    When I resemble her to thee,
How sweet and fair she seems to be.

EDWARD WALLER

Snapdragon

PRESUMPTION

Garden varieties of the snapdragon have been developed from a perennial plant of Mediterranean countries. There are varieties in most colors except shades of blues. The flowers, of which there are many growing on one stalk, look like the open jaws of an animal, explaining the plant's name. The snapdragon is aptly symbolic of "presumption" since it is a plant that will take over the garden unless it is carefully cultivated.

Snowdrop
~
HOPE
CONSOLATION

This sweet milk-white flower is said to have been created in the Garden of Eden. An angel, who was consoling Eve about the barrenness of Eden in winter, caught a falling snowflake, blew gently on it, and bade it take the form of a flower and flourish forever. Today the snowdrop is always the first flower of spring and assures us that winter will soon end. This explains why it symbolizes "hope" and "consolation."

The snowdrop, Winters timid child,
Awakens to life, bedewed with tears,
And flings around its fragrance mild;
And, where no rival flowerets bloom
Amidst the bare and chilling gloom,
A beauteous gem appears.

AUTHOR UNKNOWN

Stock
~
LASTING BEAUTY

Fair is the gillyflower of garden sweet.
JOHN GAY

Lavish stock that scents the garden round.
JOHN THOMPSON

The stock has been long established in gardens, and, under the somewhat puzzling name of "gillyflower," is frequently extolled by poets. No matter what it is called, this flower, which is less graceful than the rose and less elegant than the lily, has a splendor that is far more durable. It offers, during its very long blooming season, beautiful pyramidal flowers that have a pleasant perfume. Some people claim that the finest stock are red, but they are certainly rivaled in brilliance by those that are purple or violet. And there is much to recommend those flowers that have almost opalescent variegations.

The sunflower originated in Peru. Its flowers were used by the ancient Peruvians in their ceremonies to worship the god of day. Young maidens of the sun, who officiated at the feasts, wore golden replicas of the sunflower and carried them in their hands, too. The Spanish conquerors were astonished by this display of gold, but were still more amazed when, in May, they saw the fields covered with these same golden flowers. They were impressed that the goldsmiths could so closely replicate these splendid flowers and seemed to admire the workmanship more than the precious metal of which they were made. This seems a logical explanation for the sunflower signifying "false riches."

Sunflower
~
FALSE RICHES

Ah, Sunflower, weary of time,
Who countest the steps of the sun;
Seeking after that sweet golden clime,
Where the traveler's journey is done;

Where the youth pined away with desire,
And the pale virgin shrouded in snow,
Arise from their graves, and aspire
Where my Sunflower wished to go!
WILLIAM BLAKE

Light-enchanted sunflower, thou
Who gazest ever true and tender
On the sun's revolving splendor.
CALDERON
(TRANSLATED BY PERCY BYSSHE SHELLEY)

Sweet Pea

~

LASTING PLEASURE

DEPARTURE

This delicate, richly scented flower has an elegant, rather nonchalant shape. On one stalk the flowers may be variegated shades of blue, lilac, rose, and white. In England, the sweet pea was particularly popular during Edwardian times. It symbolizes lasting pleasure because of its fragrance and the ability of the flowers to continually renew themselves.

Here are sweet peas, on tiptoe for a flight;
With wings of gently flush o'er delicate white,
And taper fingers catching at all things,
To bind them all about with tiny rings.

JOHN KEATS

Its beauty and elegance have quite properly made the sweet William, sometimes called phlox, the emblem of gallantry and finesse. A member of the same family as the pink and the carnation, sweet William's variegated blossoms are arranged in bouquet-like clusters on each stalk. One poet described the sweet William as "Flora's color palette, on which she had frolicked, varying her favorite dyes to display all her gayest tints of reds and purples, mingled with pure white and jet black, disposed in stars. . . ."

Sweet William small has form and aspect bright,
Like that sweet flower that yields great Jove delight.
ABRAHAM COWLEY

Sweet William

~

GALLANTRY

FINESSE

Thistle
~
RETALIATION

Since the reign of James III the thistle has been the national emblem of Scotland. According to legend, one night, when a party of invading Norsemen was about to mount a surprise attack on the sleeping Scots, one of the invaders stepped on a prickly thistle. His cry of pain was so loud that it woke the Scots, who defended themselves and drove the enemy from the field. Thereafter, the thistle signified "retaliation" and it was the inspiration for Scotland's motto: *Nemo me impune lacessit*–No one shall provoke me with impunity. Those who wear the thistle are said to be protected. To dream of being surrounded by thistles is considered a good omen, a prophecy of joyous news.

Up wi' the flowers o' Scotland,
   The emblems o' the free,
Their guardians for a thousand years,
   Their guardians still we'll be.
A foe had better brave the de'il
   Within his reeky cell,
Than our thistle's purple bonnet,
   Or bonny heather bell.

JAMES HOGG

Tulip
~
DECLARATION OF LOVE

The tulip originated in the East and was worshipped by the Turks, who never ceased to admire the gorgeous hues of gold, purple, lilac, and violet, of deep crimson and delicate pink, with every possible variety of tint. The flower's name derives from *tulipan*, the Turkish word for turban, because of the similarity of its shape. The tulip was said to protect anyone who cultivated it. It was believed that these flowers were special to fairies and elves, who sat beneath them when they sang their babies to sleep.

The tulip had its worshippers in other parts of the world, too. They were quickly accepted in Europe. In Holland, from 1644 until 1647, the country was overcome by tulipomania. In these years tulip bulbs fetched enormous prices and made many speculators wealthy. To the Victorians, when a man presented a red tulip to his beloved it declared that she was so beautiful that if he saw her only for a moment his face would be as fire and his heart reduced to a coal.

Dutch tulips from their beds
Flaunted their stately heads.
JAMES MONTGOMERY

Guarded within the old red wall's embrace,
Marshalled like soldiers in gay company,
The tulips stand arrayed. Here infantry
Wheels out into the sunlight.
AMY LOWELL

Violet

~

MODESTY

FAITHFULNESS

The violet, considered by some to be the emblem of "modesty," to many others signifies "faithfulness." This timid little blossom holds an exalted place in floral calligraphy. The Greeks chose this ancient sweet-scented bloom to be the flower of Aphrodite, the goddess of love and beauty. The plant has, of course, also been associated with modesty—the reason that a shy young woman is frequently called a "shrinking violet."

The violet was Napoleon Bonaparte's favorite flower. When he was in exile in Elba the little blossom was adopted by his followers as an emblem. A small bunch of violets hung in a French home or worn by a French man or woman identified Napoleon's supporters to one another.

To famous poets, from Homer to Tennyson, the beauty and the fragrance of the violet have suggested many lovely ideas.

Violet is for faithfulness.
  Which in me shall abide:
Hoping likewise that from your heart
  You will not let it slide.
                          AUTHOR UNKNOWN

Dear violets, you liken to
The kindest eyes that look on you
  Without a thought disloyal.
              ELIZABETH BARRETT BROWNING

We are violets blue,
  For our sweetness found
Careless in the mossy shades,
  Looking on the ground.
Love's dropped eyelids and a kiss,
  Such our breath and blueness is.
                          LEIGH HUNT

The smell of violets, hidden in the green,
  Pour'd back into my empty soul and frame
The times when I remembered to have been
  Joyful and free from blame.
                    ALFRED, LORD TENNYSON

Water Lily

~

ELOQUENCE

Broad water lilies lay tremulously,
And starry river-buds glimmered by,
And around them the soft stream
*   did glide and dance,*
With a motion of sweet sound
*   and radiance.*

PERCY BYSSHE SHELLEY

The slender water lily
*   Peeps dreamingly out of the lake;*
The moon, oppress'd with love's sorrow,
*   Looks tenderly down for her sake.*

HEINRICH HEINE

The Egyptians consecrated the water lily to the sun, the god of eloquence. This enchanting flower closes at night and sleeps on the bosom of the still water from the setting of the sun until its rising the next morning. Water lilies are interwoven in the headdress of the Egyptian god Osiris. Many of the gods in the Hindu pantheon, too, are represented seated on this flower, an allusion to the legend of the world rising from the midst of the waters.

The zinnia, which was named after Johan G. Zinn, a German botanist, comes from Mexico and was brought to Europe almost two hundred years ago. The flowers are long-lived and have been developed in a wide range of wonderful bright colors. Unfortunately, it is not known why this showy flower became emblematic of "thoughts of absent friends."

Zinnia

~

THOUGHTS OF ABSENT FRIENDS

The zinnia's solitary flower,
Which blooms in forests lone and deep,
Are like the visions fair and bright,
That faithful, absent hearts will keep.

AUTHOR UNKNOWN

Saying It with Flowers
~

When a love letter might seem inadequate to convey deep, heartfelt feelings, a floral message can, even today, be the perfect solution. Arrangements of flowers, each with a distinct meaning, have long been effectively relied upon by lovers, friends, and relatives to communicate unspoken thoughts and emotions.

The Victorians were delighted with the concept of expressing sentiments of the heart with bouquets of ingeniously selected flowers. The bouquet top left, for example, signifies "beauty, friendship, and love," since it is made up of a rose, some ivy, and myrtle. The flowers on the left—broom, borage, and geranium—express the rather wordy compliment: "Bluntness of manner often accompanies a character worthy of admiration."

Lady Mary Wortley Montagu, the wife of the British ambassador to Constantinople, is said to have introduced the Eastern concept of floral language to England in 1717 when she sent a Turkish love letter to a friend. The items enclosed were a

clove, a jonquil, a pear, a rose, a piece
of straw, a stick of cinnamon, and a
few peppercorns. From these flowers,
fruit, and spices some rather arcane
botanical emblems were extracted:

Clove:

"You are as slender as this clove,
You are an unblown rose!
I have long loved you, and
you have not known it."

Jonquil:

"Have pity on my passion!"

Pear:

"Give me some hope!"

Rose:

"May you be pleased, and
your sorrows mine!"

A Piece of Straw:

"Suffer me to be your slave!"

A Stick of Cinnamon:

"But my fortune is yours!"

Peppercorns:

"Send me an answer!"

Today, depending of course upon
the character of the message intended
to be conveyed, upon the variety of
flowers that are obtainable, and upon
the ingenuity of the sender, it is possible to express a wide variety of far
simpler sentiments using the language
of flowers.

The lovely flowers top right—a tulip,
a lily, and fuchsia—express the sentiment: "Purity of taste commands admiration." It is a simple bouquet and an
appropriate message for a wonderful
host, or, perhaps, a colleague or an older
relative. The flowers right, are perfect to
send to a friend, although they might

not be easy to obtain. The combination of trumpet flowers, forget me nots, and blackberry brambles says: "When friends separate, they desire mutual remembrance."

Similarly, a message that conveys the desire to be united in the bonds of marriage can be easily expressed with a bouquet of blue convolvulus to indicate "a bond," ivy, which represents "marriage," and a few pieces of straw to signify "union." If a man wants to tell a woman that her friendliness gives him hope of one day having her love, he might send her a floral arrangement of acacia, signifying "friendship," snowdrops or hawthorn, emblems of "hope," and myrtle or red roses, indicative of "love."

The flowers top left—white jasmine, a China rose, a pink, and a purple violet—convey the rather elaborate, and stuffy, message: "Amiability and modesty secure a lively and enduring affection, and constitute a perpetual loveliness." The flowers left—thrift, dog rose, and broom—together signify "True sympathy is a characteristic of the simple-hearted," a sentiment that might not be considered a compliment.

A bouquet of delicate, fragrant mignonette signifies: "Your qualities surpass your charms," another compliment that might be questioned by the recipient. The significance of the mignonette goes back to the days of the Count of Walstheim, a Saxon nobleman. He was in love with Amelia, a beautiful, flirtatious heiress. Then one evening at a party, she chose a beautiful red rose as her personal emblem. Her cousin Charlotte, who was neither wealthy nor beautiful (but was certainly amiable and quite intelligent), picked as her emblem a modest spray of mignonette. The Count, realizing that sincere affection and charm were far more precious than superficial beauty and gaiety, married Charlotte and added a branch of mignonette to his heraldic coat of arms with the motto: *Ses qualites surpassent ses charmes.* The bouquet bottom right expands the motto. Composed of mignonette, heliotrope, and a pink, it says: "Your qualities surpass your charms; my affection marks the distinction." The sentiment of the flowers shown right is rather bewildering. The flowers are nightshade, heath, and bindweed (none of which is easily obtained). They state: "Truth is humble and retiring."

It is really not difficult to send floral messages to express your feelings. A bouquet of holly and mistletoe declares: "With foresight you will surmount your difficulties." The significance of a little nosegay of scented violets, white jasmine, and moss roses is: "Your modesty and amiability inspire me with the warmest affection." And, of course, a single red rose is the simplest way to say: "I love you."

The Floral Dictionary

~

The Language of Fruits and Vegetables

~

Apple   Temptation
Cabbage   Gain, Profit
Chicory   Frugality
Citron   Ill-natured Beauty
Corn   Riches
Cranberry   Hardness
          Cure for Heartache
Cucumber   Criticism
Currant   Thy Frown Will Kill Me
Endive   Frugality
Fig   Longevity
Gooseberry   Anticipation
Grape   Intemperance
Lemon   Zest
Lettuce   Cold-heartedness
Mushroom   Suspicion
Oats   The Witching Soul of Music
Olive   Peace
Peach   Your Qualities Like Your
          Charms are Unequalled
Pear   Affection
Persimmon   Bury Me Amid
              Nature's Beauties
Pineapple   Perfection
Pomegranate   Foolishness
Potato   Benevolence
Prickly Pear   Satire
Pumpkin   Coarseness
Raspberry   Remorse
Rhubarb   Advice
Strawberry   Excellence
Sweet Pea   Departure
             Lasting Pleasures
Turnip   Charity
Walnut   Intellect
Watermelon   Bulk
Wheat   Wealth
Wild Grape   Charity

The Language of Herbs and Spices

~

Allspice   Compassion

Aloe   Bitterness, Grief

      Religious Superstition

Angelica   Inspiration

Basil   Hatred

Bay Leaf   I Change But in Death

Borage   Bluntness

Camomile   Energy in Adversity

Cinnamon   Forgiveness of Injuries

Clove   Dignity

Coriander   Hidden Merit

Fennel   Force, Strength

      Worthy of All Praise

Hyssop   Cleanliness

Juniper   Protection

Licorice   I Declare Against You

Majoram   Blushes

Mint   Virtue

Mustard Seed   Indifference

Parsley   Banquet, Festivity

Peppermint   Cordiality

      Warmth of Sentiment

Rosemary   Remembrance

      Your Presence Revives Me

Rue   Repentance

Saffron   Marriage

Sage   Domestic Virtue

      Esteem

Sorrel   Parental Affection

      Returned Affection

Sweet Basil   Good Wishes

Thyme   Thriftiness

Veleria   Accommodating Disposition

Wormwood   Absence

The Language
of Trees

~

Acadia Chaste Love

Almond Stupidity

American Elm Patriotism

American Laurel Virtue is Charming

American Linden Matrimony

Ash Grandeur

Aspen Lamentation

Balsam Ardent Love

Bay Glory

Beech Prosperity

Birch Grace
　　　Meekness

Black Mulberry I Will Not Survive You

Black Pine Pity

Black Poplar Courage

Bladdernut Frivolity
　　　　Amusement

Box Stoicism

Cedar Constancy in Love
　　　Strength

Cedar of Lebanon Incorruptible

Cherry Good Education

Chestnut Do Me Justice

Cinnamon Forgiveness of Injuries

Creeping Willow Love Forsaken

Cypress Death
　　　Despair
　　　Mourning

Dogwood Duration

Ebony Blackness

Elm Dignity

Evergreen Poverty

Fig Profuseness
　　Prolific
Fir Elevation
　　Time
French Willow Bravery and Humanity
Hazel Reconciliation
Herb Willow Pretension
Holly Foresight
Judas Betrayal
　　Unbelief
Laurel Victory
　　Glory
Linden Conjugal Love
Live Oak Liberty
Locust Affection Beyond the Grave
　　Elegance
Magnolia Love of Nature
　　　Magnificence
Laurel-leaved Magnolia Dignity
Maple Reserve
Mimosa Sensitiveness
Mountain Ash Prudence
Mountain Laurel Ambition
Oak Hospitality
Orange Generosity
Palm Victory
Pear Comfort
Pine Daring
　　Endurance
Pitch Pine Time and Faith
Plane Genius

Plum Fidelity
        Keep Your Promises
Red Balsam Impatient Resolves
Spruce Farewell
        Hope in Adversity
Swamp Magnolia Perseverance
Sycamore Curiosity
        Reserve
Thorn Apple Deceitful Charms
Thorn Evergreen Solace in Adversity
Tulip Fame
Walnut Intellect
        Stratagem
Water Willow Freedom
Weeping Willow Melancholy
        Mourning
White Cherry Deception
White Mulberry Wisdom
White Poplar Time
Yellow Balsam Impatience